ORGANIZING AND USING INFORMATION

Beth A. Pulver and Donald C. Adcock

Heinemann Library
Chicago, Illinois

Customer Service 888-454-2279
Visit our website at www.heinemannraintree.com

Design: Richard Parker and Tinstar Design Ltd.
Photo research: Fiona Orbell and Elizabeth Alexander

Origination by Chroma Graphics (Overseas) Pte. Ltd.
Printed and bound in China by Leo Paper Products Ltd

ISBN: 978-1-4329-1229-1 (hc)

13 12 11
10 9 8 7 6 5 4 3 2

Library of Congress Cataloging-in-Publication Data
Pulver, Beth A.
  Organizing and using information / Beth A. Pulver and Donald C. Adcock.
       p. cm. -- (Information literacy skills)
  Includes bibliographical references and index.
  ISBN 978-1-4329-1229-1
  1. Research--Methodology--Juvenile literature. 2. Report writing--Juvenile literature. 3. Information literacy--Juvenile literature. I. Adcock, Donald C. II. Title.
  ZA3080.P854 2008
  001.4--dc22
                        2008018730

Acknowledgments
The author and publishers are grateful to the following for permission to reproduce copyright material: © Alamy/Chuck Pefley p. **43**; © Corbis/Image Source p. **34**; © Creatas p. **35**; © Getty Images pp. /Adam Gault **21**, /David Silverman **25**, /Keith Brofsky **36**, /Lenora Gim **4**, /Paul Thomas **40**; © iStockphoto pp. /Damir Karan **30**, /Mark Stout **7**; © PhotoDisc/Photolink/S. Meltzer **26**.

Background features and cover photograph reproduced with permission of © iStockphoto.

Contents

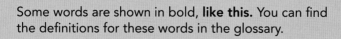

Some words are shown in bold, **like this.** You can find the definitions for these words in the glossary.

Getting Organized

You receive information every day. If you went to school today, you had several classes and learned hundreds of pieces of information. If you read a book, watched TV, or surfed the Web you received information. If you talked to your parents or friends, you got even more information. The question is, what do you do with all of this information?

When you are trying to answer a specific question or writing a research paper, you need to find effective ways of organizing this information so that you can use it. The better organized you are when collecting information and taking notes, the easier it will be to use your information. Good organization of your information will help you to clearly express the answer to the question.

Being well organized makes it easier to find things, saves time, and makes it more likely that you will come up with the correct answer or solution to your question or problem.

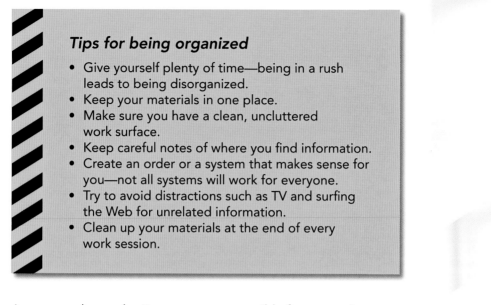

Tips for being organized

- Give yourself plenty of time—being in a rush leads to being disorganized.
- Keep your materials in one place.
- Make sure you have a clean, uncluttered work surface.
- Keep careful notes of where you find information.
- Create an order or a system that makes sense for you—not all systems will work for everyone.
- Try to avoid distractions such as TV and surfing the Web for unrelated information.
- Clean up your materials at the end of every work session.

As a researcher and writer, you are responsible for presenting or using your information in the correct way. Different types of information require different presentations. In this book we will look at some different strategies for organizing your information, as well as ways to use or present that information.

Asking a question

Sometimes the best way to start a research project is to ask a question. A question will help guide you in finding the information you need. Some people refer to this question as a research question or a problem statement.

For some questions you will just need a one-word or one-sentence answer. Complicated questions or assignments may require looking at many different magazines, books, or journals. You may want to use the Internet or other electronic sources, such as online **databases**, to locate the information needed to answer your questions or provide solutions to your problems. The more complex the question or problem, the more sources you are likely to need to examine. Being well organized will make these more complicated questions easier to answer.

Using graphic organizers

Graphic organizers are tools to help you organize your facts so that you can communicate with your audience. Graphic organizers can be used in all subject areas that you study in school. They can also be used outside of school to help you organize information to make decisions or solve problems.

Sometimes, before you begin doing research, you need a way to organize the information. A **KWL** chart can be very helpful in all stages of your research. K stands for <u>K</u>now, W stands for <u>W</u>ant to know, and L stands for what you <u>L</u>earn in your research. The first two columns are filled in before your research starts, and the last is filled in as you work. A KWL chart will help you sort out the facts you learned during the research process from those you already knew on the topic. It will also help you come to a conclusion when you fill in the "What I Learned" section of the chart.

Using a KWL chart will help you combine the information you already knew with the information you found and learned from. Using your facts will require that you use **critical thinking** or **problem solving** skills to answer your question or solve your problem. After you have determined your answer or solution, you will then need to communicate the answer or solution to your audience.

A KWL chart

Topic: Reference materials
Question: How can I do research?

What I <u>K</u>now	What I <u>W</u>ant to know	What I <u>L</u>earned
Libraries have different types of reference materials. The Internet can be a good source of information	Is the Internet trustworthy for research? How can I tell if an author is reliable?	It is important to verify information in more than one source. Sometimes books are quicker than the Internet. It is important to learn how to tell if an author is **biased**.

Different learning styles

Everyone has a different way in which they best learn. Some people learn best when listening to words, others learn best when reading words. Some people prefer to see things visually. Imagine you are trying to find out how to get to a friend's house. Do you prefer to be given directions, or would you rather look at a map? If you would rather look at a map, you may be a visual learner.

The first step to being able to use information properly is organizing it. A jumble of disorganized information can lead to errors.

Visual organizers

Visual organizers can be especially helpful for people who are visual learners. They organize written information in a **graphic** form. Visual organizers use geometric shapes like circles, rectangles, or squares. Some popular forms of visual organizers are **concept webs**, **Venn diagrams**, timelines, **fishbone maps**, **flowcharts**, and story maps. Each of these graphic organizers helps the user organize information. They are used in science, history, language arts, and math. They are tools that you can use anytime in your life to help you organize information or make decisions.

Venn diagrams

Venn diagrams were invented in 1881 by a mathematician named John Venn. They are especially useful for comparing and contrasting information. Below is the basic outline of a Venn diagram. Imagine you are studying household pets. You might label the left circle "cats" and the circle on the right "dogs." In each circle you would list unique aspects of each animal. In the middle you would list things the animals have in common, such as "mammals" or "come in several breeds." If you wanted to add a third animal, you would simply draw a third circle, making sure it overlaps with the first two circles at some point. The second example shows three pets and some of the attributes they have in common.

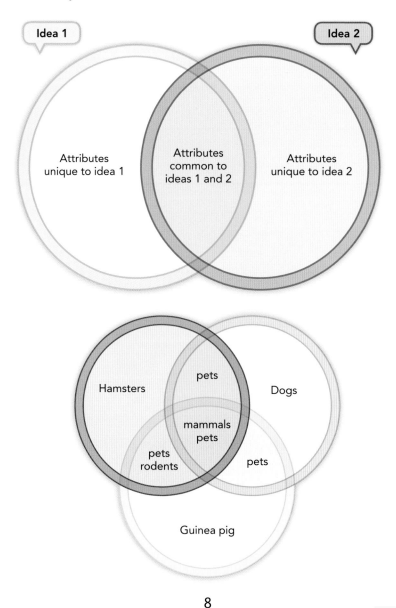

Idea 1

Idea 2

Attributes unique to idea 1

Attributes common to ideas 1 and 2

Attributes unique to idea 2

Hamsters

pets

Dogs

mammals
pets

pets
rodents

pets

Guinea pig

Timeline of the development of the Massachusetts Colony

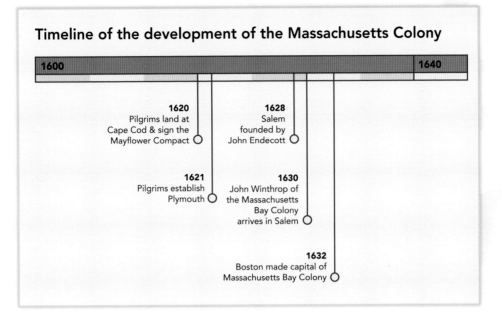

| 1600 | | 1640 |

1620
Pilgrims land at
Cape Cod & sign the
Mayflower Compact

1628
Salem
founded by
John Endecott

1621
Pilgrims establish
Plymouth

1630
John Winthrop of
the Massachusetts
Bay Colony
arrives in Salem

1632
Boston made capital of
Massachusetts Bay Colony

Timeline of the development of the Virginia Colony

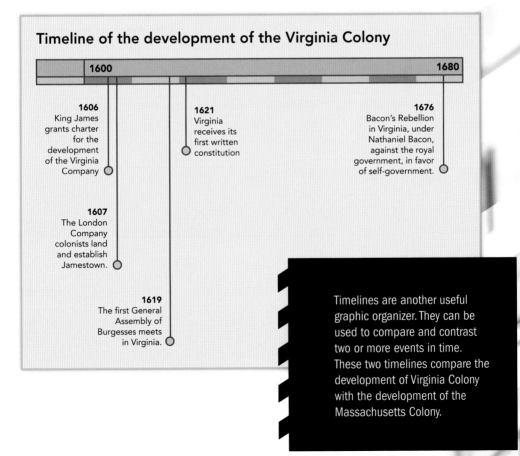

| 1600 | | 1680 |

1606
King James
grants charter
for the
development
of the Virginia
Company

1621
Virginia
receives its
first written
constitution

1676
Bacon's Rebellion
in Virginia, under
Nathaniel Bacon,
against the royal
government, in favor
of self-government.

1607
The London
Company
colonists land
and establish
Jamestown.

1619
The first General
Assembly of
Burgesses meets
in Virginia.

Timelines are another useful graphic organizer. They can be used to compare and contrast two or more events in time. These two timelines compare the development of Virginia Colony with the development of the Massachusetts Colony.

Fishbone maps

A fishbone map, also known as a fishbone diagram or herringbone map, can be useful in organizing information. These diagrams are especially useful if your research topic has many different facets. To fill in the fishbone, place the main idea in the middle. Each bone, or line, will contain a major attribute or point about the main idea. Then fill in the smaller sections with facts about the attributes.

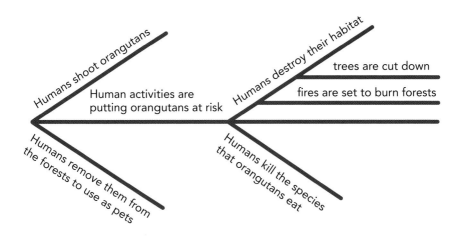

Using a concept web

When using a concept web, the center circle contains your research question. Each main branch will become your main idea. Each main idea branch will have other branches, or subheadings. These subheading bubbles will be your branches, with bubbles containing supporting facts or details. These facts may come from your KWL chart. You will include the facts you already knew on the subject from column one and the facts you learned during the research process from the third column.

Imagine a class of 8th-grade students studying the endangered species of Central America. The students are given a list of animals and plants to select from. One student selects the elfin tree fern, an endangered plant found in several Central American countries. This is a topic the student only knows a little about, so she doesn't have many facts in the first column of her KWL chart. The student finds many facts about this plant during the research process. She finds facts about the elfin tree fern, its habitat, and why the plant is on the endangered species list. By organizing the facts in the concept web, the student is now ready to write an answer to the question "Why is the elfin tree fern on the endangered species list?" The facts already known are mixed in with the facts learned during the research process. Below is an example of the concept map for the research question "Why is the elfin tree fern an endangered species in Central America?"

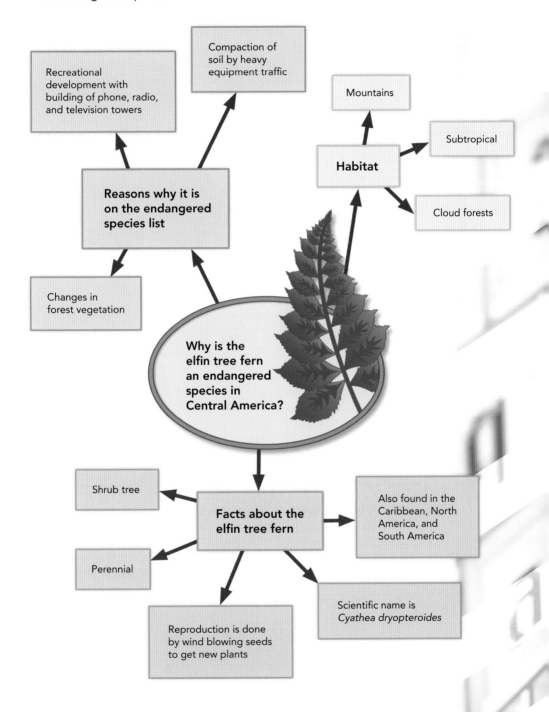

The problem-solving model

Like the concept web, the **problem-solving model** will help you arrange your facts. By organizing the facts in the problem-solving model, you are able to state a solution to the problem and present that solution to your audience. In the "problem" box, you will state the problem. The "possible solution" boxes will be filled in with possible solutions based on the facts you found in your research. You will use the facts you already knew on the topic and those you found during the research process. The "possible result" boxes will be filled in across from each possible solution with a possible result or consequence. The conclusion box will be filled in by you drawing a conclusion from each of the possible solutions and their consequences. By drawing a conclusion, you will present your own explanation of the solution to the problem and any consequences.

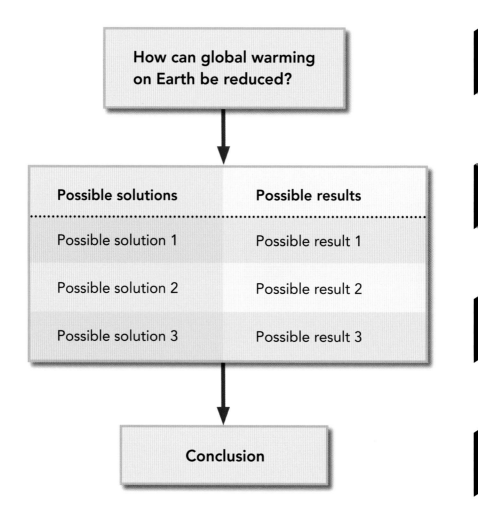

How can global warming on Earth be reduced?

Possible solutions	Possible results
Possible solution 1	Possible result 1
Possible solution 2	Possible result 2
Possible solution 3	Possible result 3

Conclusion

Using graphic outlines

We all have different ways of using information to answer questions or solve problems. If you are not a visual learner, you may not find graphic organizers easy to use. You may prefer to organize your information by using a **graphic outline**. Graphic outlines are used to organize information, but instead of being a visual organization of your facts, it is an organized list arranged by topic and subtopic. Graphic outlines begin by stating the problem to be solved or the question to be answered. This would look like a title for the outline. Graphic outlines use a combination of **Roman numerals**, letters, and **Arabic numbers** to represent each topic, subtopic, and supporting details. The Roman numerals are used to indicate your main ideas.

What are Roman numerals?

Roman numerals are numerical symbols used by the ancient Romans.

Examples:

I = 1	VIII = 8	L = 50
II = 2	IX = 9	C = 100
IV = 4	X = 10	D = 500
V = 5	XX = 20	M = 1,000
VI = 6	XXI = 21	
VII = 7	XL = 40	

Using the example of the student researching elfin tree ferns, the main ideas are facts about the elfin tree fern, the habitat of the elfin tree fern, and reasons why the elfin tree fern is on the endangered species list. Each main idea would be represented by Roman numerals I, II, and III, and are also the same as the main idea bubbles in the concept web. The subheadings for each heading are represented by a capital or upper-case letter. Supporting facts and details are represented by the Arabic numbers 1 and 2 (see p.14).

Why is the elfin tree fern an endangered species in Central America?

I. The elfin tree fern grows in the subtropics of Central America.
  A. The elfin tree fern requires a subtropical habitat to grow.
    1. Cloud forests create the moisture needed for the growth of the tree.
    2. The cloud forests are located high in the mountains.

  B. The elfin tree fern is located in two countries of Central America.
    1. Costa Rica is located between Nicaragua and Panama.
    2. Nicaragua is located between the Caribbean Sea and the Pacific Ocean.

II. The elfin tree fern is a unique tree.
  A. The elfin tree fern belongs to the tree family and not the fern family.
    1. It is a shrub tree.
    2. It is a perennial.

  B. Reproduction of the elfin tree fern is done with seeds.
    1. Seeds are spread by wind blowing them to get new plants.
    2. The seeds must land on fertile soil.

  C. There are other facts about the elfin tree fern.
    1. Its scientific name is _Cyathea dryopteroides_.
    2. They are also found in the Caribbean, North America, and South America.

III. There are two reasons why the elfin tree fern is on the endangered species list.
  A. Humans have changed the environment that the tree grows in.
    1. They have built phone, radio, and television towers in the mountains where the tree grows.
    2. There has been compaction of soil by heavy equipment traffic where the towers were built.

  B. Other changes in the environment have endangered the trees.
    1. The forest vegetation has changed because of global warming.
    2. Global warming has caused changes in the climate.

This graphic outline uses complete sentences to arrange the topics, subtopics, and supporting details for the research question.

Key words and sentences

When you are developing your graphic outline, you combine the facts you already knew with the facts you learned during the research process. When using a graphic outline, every main idea, or Roman numeral, must have at least two subheadings or upper-case letters. Every subheading or upper-case letter must have at least two supporting facts or details. If you cannot fill these in, then your main points may not be large enough to justify being main points.

There are two methods of using a graphic outline. One method uses complete sentences for each topic, subtopic, and supporting facts and details in the outline. The other method uses key words for each topic, subtopic, and supporting facts and details in the outline. The advantage of using the complete sentence method is that when it is time to write the rough draft of your presentation, most of the writing is already done. When using the complete sentence method, you must be careful to put the information down in your own words and not copy from the source you are using. Advantages to using the key-word method are that it is easier to add in new facts, and you are more likely to use your own words when writing the draft copy of your presentation.

You may fill out a graphic outline, or any other visual organizer, and discover that your topic no longer seems to make sense. Perhaps the conclusions you thought were true at the beginning have changed. Perhaps there simply isn't as much information as you thought. This can be frustrating, but it is important to remember that these steps are all part of the research and writing process. This is another reason to not leave research and writing until the last minute. The process can take time and can have many false starts.

You may also find it easier to organize your thoughts if you are not trying to form complete sentences. Depending on how comfortable you are with your writing skills, trying to organize your thoughts and write your paper at the same time may be difficult for you.

Taking Notes

Using note cards is a way to organize your information as you prepare your presentation for an audience. Examples of the type of presentation you could be making are a written paper, a computer-generated presentation, or a poster. Some presentations of your information may be done in the form of an oral report, or it may be a part of the presentation that goes with a poster.

Source cards

A helpful card to create is a source card. This card will be used when creating your **bibliography.** A bibliography is a list of the sources used in researching a topic. As you prepare your paragraph, essay, or presentation, you will want to make sure that you give credit to the authors who provided you with your facts. If a fact was one you already knew before your research, you do not need to tell where the information came from. If you got the information from a source like a book, magazine, newspaper, video, or website, you must provide information about that source. This is your bibliography. You may also use quotations within your paragraph, essay, or presentation as a way to give credit to the authors providing your facts. If you use quotes, you must still include that source in your bibliography.

Your source card should have the author and title of the source. It should also have the name of the publisher or producer, and the date and place of the publication or production. This information can usually be found on the **imprint page** of a book. Each source card should be labeled with an upper-case letter in the upper left-hand corner of the card.

Fact cards

After creating source cards, you will want to create fact cards. Each fact card should have only one fact on it. You should find a way to label each card indicating what source the information comes from. For example, label your first source card with the letter A. Then label each fact card from that source with a letter A. Another option would be to use different colors for each source.

Handyside, Christopher. Jazz.

    Chicago: Heinemann Library, 2006.

Jazz music began in New Orleans, Louisiana, as early as the 1890s.

Handyside, Christopher. Jazz.

    Chicago: Heinemann Library, 2006.

"Parker's playing style was more personal and expressive than that of other saxophonists. He seemed to be playing not out of a need to entertain, but purely to express himself."

Paraphrases and summaries

There are three types of information written on fact cards. They are **paraphrases, summaries**, and direct quotations. A paraphrase is the restatement of a fact found in one of your sources that you have put into your own words. A summary is a sentence that combines the information found in several sentences into one statement of fact. Direct quotations are statements taken directly from the source without changing any of the words.

Direct quotations must begin and end with quotation marks to show that they are not your words, but those of the author. When using a direct quotation, it is very important that you make sure you have quoted the author correctly. Do not leave out any words or change words, even if the author has made a mistake. If you do so, you could change the author's ideas.

Is it plagiarism?

Plagiarism is using someone else's ideas and information as if they are your own. If you take facts from a source, that could be plagiarism. It is acceptable to use information, facts, and even opinions found in other books. However, you must **cite** them in the bibliography, **footnotes**, or **endnotes** (see pages 38–39 for more information).

Plagiarism is not the use of common facts that everyone knows.

Fact taken from a source
At the mouth of the Amazon River, 4.2 million cubic feet of water empties into the ocean per second. (Taken from "How Great is the Amazon River," http://www.extremescience.com/AmazonRiver.htm)

Common known fact
The Amazon River in South America is the largest river in the world by volume.

Paraphrase

Paraphrases are restatements of information put into your own words.

Text:

"The Troubles are rooted in the split between the Protestant and Catholic communities, which can be traced back at least four hundred years."

Paraphrased text:

The split between Protestants and Catholics can be traced back four hundred years.

Summarize

A summary combines information into fewer words.

Text:

"Following an unsuccessful rebellion against British rule, Scottish Protestant settlers were deliberately moved to Ireland on the orders of the British king. They were "planted," or settled in Ulster, the region where the rebellion had been centered."

Summarized text:

The British king moved Scottish Protestant settlers to Ulster, a region of Ireland.

Text taken from *The Troubles in Northern Ireland* by Tony Allan, Heinemann Library, 2004.

You use direct quotations to provide support for the point of view being expressed in your presentation. You may also use direct quotations to provide context for your thoughts. Another reason to use a direct quotation is when the author has phrased something so well that you know you could not do a better job of it yourself.

It is important that you keep careful track of what you are paraphrasing, summarizing, and quoting. You do not want to accidentally copy someone else's work and ideas without the proper citation or credit for them. That would be plagiarism.

Tips for taking good notes

- When taking notes, you will be looking at many sources of information. It is important to make sure that the information you are writing in your notes relates to the topic you will be writing about. You will want to refer back to your original research question to make sure the information is related to your topic before writing it down on a note card.

- When you find a piece of information that you want to include on a note card, it is very important that you make sure to write the letter of the source from your source card. Then write the number of the page on which the piece of information is located before you go on to the next note card. If you do not do this, you will not be able to go back to the source if you need to verify the information.

- All the information on the note cards should be placed in the same location on the card.

- Source cards should have a letter in the upper left-hand corner and information such as the author, title, publisher, and date on the card.

- Fact note cards should have the source letter in the upper left-hand corner, page numbers in the upper right-hand corner, and a single statement of fact per card.

- After you have taken your notes, you need to determine if you have enough relevant information to answer your question or solve your problem. You will take the fact note cards and sort them by topic and then subtopic by referring back to your graphic organizer or graphic outline. This will help you see where you might need more information. It will also help you see what fact cards are not related to the question or problem to be solved, and you can discard those fact note cards from your piles.

Working in a clean, comfortable space can help you organize your thoughts and your research.

Integrating new information

As you begin to prepare your presentation or write your paper, you will use your KWL chart to blend together the facts you already know on your topic with those facts you learned from your research. You will do this by combining the information from column one in the chart, the facts you already know, with the facts from column three, the facts you learned from the research process. Using any of the graphic organizers—the concept web, Venn diagram, timeline, or graphic outline—will help you put the information you have on your topic into categories. These categories are the headings and subheadings with supporting facts that add details to your report or presentation.

Elfin tree fern categories

I. General Information
    Scientific name, location, type of plant, life cycle
II. Information about its habitat
III. How the habitat has changed, why the tree is on the endangered species list

Once you have similar facts together, you will need to prioritize the categories and decide which category your audience must know first about your topic. When sharing with your audience, you must have a beginning, middle, and end. The beginning should describe your question or problem to be solved. The middle of your presentation is the collection of the information you have gathered during your research. The end of the presentation, or conclusion, will describe the answer to the question or solution to the problem that your research supports.

Creating a rough draft

One way to determine if you have enough information is to begin writing a **rough draft** of your paper or assignment. As you write your draft, you will start to see where you have holes and need more research. Having an organized draft will make these holes clearer. One of the best ways to organize your paper is to think about three parts, an introductory statement, or **topic sentence**, supporting detail statements, and a conclusion. Whether you have a paragraph or multiple paragraphs, it will probably follow the same format.

Paragraph graphic organizer

Main idea or topic sentence

Supporting sentence or details	Supporting sentence or details	Supporting sentence or details

Concluding sentence

For a multiple-paragraph assignment, you will have an introductory paragraph, several paragraphs containing information that supports your introduction, and a concluding paragraph that summarizes the content of your presentation. As you are completing your rough draft, you will know if you have enough information to answer your question or solve your problem. If you do not, you will need to locate more information based on what you have already gathered during your research.

Multiple-paragraph essay graphic organizer

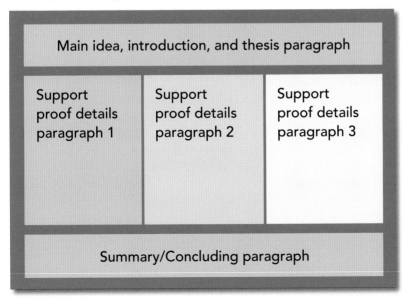

Main idea, introduction, and thesis paragraph

Support proof details paragraph 1	Support proof details paragraph 2	Support proof details paragraph 3

Summary/Concluding paragraph

Applying Information

When you find information, you must evaluate this information and decide if it is relevant. At times you may find information that does not agree with other information you have found on the topic. When you find conflicting facts, you need to verify which fact is correct by finding additional sources.

When you find conflicting information, you need to consider the source of the information. Once you know the source of the information, you must determine if the author of the information is knowledgeable about the topic. You will need to make sure that the information is up to date by determining the age of the source. Does the source that contains the conflicting fact provide a list of sources the author used? If a list is provided, you can use the list to locate an additional source to confirm which fact is correct. If there is no list provided, then you must search for additional sources that contain the same facts found in your information. As you go through this process of determining the accuracy of the facts, you are using critical-thinking skills and problem-solving skills.

A critical thinker ...

- Gathers facts to answer a question on a topic or issue.
- Analyzes facts with an open mind for accuracy and clarity.
- Draws conclusions based on facts.
- Organizes information to answer questions.
- Is able to support decisions with facts.

Critical-thinking skills

Critical thinking is the ability to analyze information and make decisions based on that information. You are thinking critically when you analyze the facts you have found with the information you already know. You then evaluate all the information and decide what the answer is. You are then able to give reasons to support your decision. Take for example a group of students assigned to research whether or not their city's recycling program is effective. The students must take a position either that the program is or is not working.

Before the students can take a position, they first must research their city's recycling program. They have to look at issues such as whether people are using it, how much it costs, and if it is environmentally correct. They should also look at the plans of other cities and towns to see how they are different. After this research has taken place, they must organize their information and prepare their arguments to take a position.

A problem such as how to recycle materials is complicated and requires critical-thinking skills.

Conclusions

The students will demonstrate their critical-thinking skills by gathering facts, reading with common sense, organizing their information, and then deciding, based on the facts, whether or not their city's plan is good. This decision requires facts and careful consideration.

You will use the skill of critical thinking in every aspect of life, not just in the classroom. It is a skill used when making purchases, applying for colleges, and even when choosing friends.

Problem-solving skills

Problem solving is the ability to define a problem, identify and prioritize possible solutions and their consequences, select a solution, and then implement that solution to resolve the problem.

Take for example a group of students studying landfills. A landfill is a place that has been filled with garbage, which is then buried. There are many possible problems with landfills. The students must come up with some solutions to reduce the amount of garbage going into landfills.

A landfill is a place where garbage is dumped and buried.

Define the problem

The students must first define or state the problem: "How can we have less garbage going into landfills?" After researching different types of garbage and how they are disposed of, the students will decide on two or three possible solutions and their consequences. In a third step, the students will decide which solution is the best possible one. They must be able to defend this solution and will use their facts to do so.

Like critical-thinking skills, the skill of problem solving is one that you will use on a daily basis in your life. You use problem-solving skills every day. For example, these skills help you learn how to solve conflicts with other people, how to fix your printer or cell phone, and how to make time for both friends and homework.

A problem solver ...

- Defines the problem.
- States possible solutions.
- States possible positive or negative consequences for each solution.
- Determines a solution for the problem.
- Defends the solution with facts.

Communicating Information

If you are very interested in your research project, it may seem like writing up a report is a waste of time. After all, you could be spending that time learning more. However, communicating your results is an important part of research.

As you organize your information, you will need to decide the best format in which to present it. Sometimes your teacher will tell you what sort of presentation you will be doing, and sometimes you will choose for yourself. The type of information you have on your research topic may also determine your format.

Written reports

When you are in school, the most common form of presentation is a written report. You have probably already done a variety of types of writing. You may have written stories, reports, and reviews. Each kind of writing has its own style and its own rules. As you progress in school and in life, you will learn many other types of writing.

Types of writing

Type	Definition	Examples
Narrative	Tells a story, can be fiction or nonfiction	Story, novel, letter, explanation, personal story, news story
Expository	Gives information, based in fact	News story, instructions, report
Persuasive	Writing meant to convince someone of your point of view	Request, book review
Scientific/Technical	Goal is to explain research or experimental findings	Medical report, research report

Some reports or papers may combine different types of writing.

Writing techniques

Depending on the goal of your writing, you will use different types of writing and different techniques. For example, imagine your goal is to persuade people in your city to recycle more. You will be writing a persuasive essay. You will be using facts, but you will be using your facts in a persuasive way. If you were writing a report on how effective the recycling program in your city is, you would use less descriptive language. Below is an example of how the same topic might look in different types of writing. Some of the information given is the same, but the style is very different. To be an effective communicator, you have to know which style is best for your subject and purpose. Here are some examples:

Persuasive: "Imagine garbage seeping out of the landfill and into your drinking water."

Expository: "Nine out of ten people do not recycle."

Narrative: "When the mayor first announced the new recycling program, citizens were excited. However, today only one out of every ten people bothers to put plastic water bottles in a recycling bin."

How good is your writing?

- Is it clear and easy to read?
- Is it free of spelling and punctuation errors?
- Is it written in an appropriate form and style?
- Is it well organized and logical?

The easiest way to improve your writing is to read and write. When you read well-written materials, you learn the rules of writing without even trying. You see how writers use different kinds of words and styles for different reasons. Any kind of reading that you do can help you to see what does and does not work in writing.

Small-group presentations

Graphs, charts, brochures, **flip books**, and written reports are best used for small groups, where they can be passed around the audience. They can also be used as part of a larger display, where the audience can view them after the presentation. These types of presentations should have enough information included on the topic that they are able to stand by themselves without an additional **oral** presentation. This means that you, as the writer, do not need to be there to explain the information contained in the product. Many different topics can be presented in graphs, charts, brochures, flip books, and written reports.

Graphs and charts

Graphs and charts are best used to present any **data** or **statistics** you may have to answer your question or solve your problem. They are also a great way to display factual support for the reasons you came to a certain conclusion. Graphs and charts are great visual ways to display facts. They may be presented by themselves, or included in larger presentations like written reports or computer-generated presentations. There are several computer programs that will help generate these graphs and charts. Examples of some software packages that create graphs and charts are Microsoft Excel, Lotus 1, 2, 3, Corel Quattro, Mariner Calc, and iWork Numbers for Macintosh. If you have statistics on a country or scientific data, your best format may be a graph or table.

Graphs and charts can come in a wide range of formats, such as the bar graphs and pie chart shown here.

Presenting online

Writing for an online audience is different from other kinds of presentations, both written and spoken. Information that will only be read online must be well written. However, because people read from a computer screen in a different way than they do a book, different rules and techniques apply. You are probably already familiar with some of these techniques from using e-mail and text messages. Although the formats may change with time, the methods you are learning today for organizing and researching information will still be helpful.

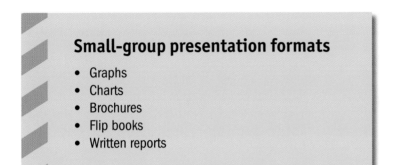

Small-group presentation formats

- Graphs
- Charts
- Brochures
- Flip books
- Written reports

Brochures

Brochures can be single fold or bifold. A single-fold brochure can be as simple as a piece of paper folded in half. A bifold brochure has two folds dividing the paper into thirds. This will give you six areas in which to present information. The front panel is generally reserved for the cover, leaving the inside flap, three interior sections, and the back panel to present information.

When presenting information in a brochure, you will use a combination of techniques. These techniques include the use of full paragraphs, bulleted lists, graphs, charts, and pictures or clip art in each section created by the folds of the paper. Brochures can be generated by hand or on a computer. There are several computer programs that will help generate these brochures. Examples of some software packages that create brochures are Microsoft Word and Publisher, Corel WordPerfect, AppleWorks, and iWork Pages.

Flip books

Flip books are created by folding sheets of paper to create pages. The folds on each page are adjusted so that tabs are created when all of the sheets are put together. Information is written on each spread of pages. The top page when all of the pages are folded closed is the cover. Flip books can be any number of pages or size depending on the number of sheets of paper used and the size of the sheets.

Large-group presentations

When you have larger audiences, you will want to use formats that are seen easily from a distance. These would include posters, trifold display boards, and computer-generated presentations that are projected onto a screen. Many different topics can be presented in these formats. Results from science experiments are often displayed on posters or three-sided display boards.

Examples of large-group presentation formats

- Posters
- Trifold display boards
- Computer-generated slide show projected onto a screen

Oral presentations

There are two different types of oral presentations, formal and informal. Formal oral presentations are done when presenting written reports as a speech or when conducting a debate. Written reports are often presented to your classmates in the form of a speech. For many of these presentations, you stand in front of your classmates at the front of the classroom and present your facts and the answer to your question or solution to your problem.

Debates

Debates are another way to present information. Debates require at least two peope, and each person has taken a side on the question or problem. During a debate the participants have the chance to express their views with supporting facts. After each participant has presented a position, the other participant has a chance to offer a rebuttal to that point of view. At the end of the debate, the participants have a chance to conclude or summarize their point of view.

Appropriate presentation formats for specific types of information

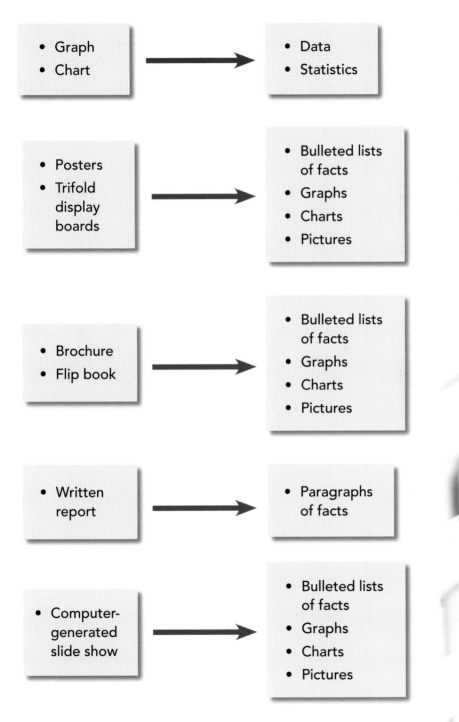

- Graph
- Chart

→

- Data
- Statistics

- Posters
- Trifold display boards

→

- Bulleted lists of facts
- Graphs
- Charts
- Pictures

- Brochure
- Flip book

→

- Bulleted lists of facts
- Graphs
- Charts
- Pictures

- Written report

→

- Paragraphs of facts

- Computer-generated slide show

→

- Bulleted lists of facts
- Graphs
- Charts
- Pictures

Both speeches and debates are usually written in the form of a paper or essay. For the actual presentation, the participants may have cards with notes from their paper or essay to use during the speech or debate. They may have visual aides like posters, graphs, charts, pictures, or brochures on hand to use during their presentation.

Formal presentations

Formal oral presentations may be done using computer-generated presentation software. There are several computer programs that will help you generate slide presentations. Examples of some software packages that create presentation slides are Microsoft PowerPoint, Corel Presentations, Lotus Freelance Graphics, and iWork Keynote. When using presentation software, your slides should not have complete sentences or paragraphs. The information included on each slide should be enough for your audience to follow your presentation, but not so much that the audience can read ahead.

Debating skills will help you throughout your life.

Studying Insects

- What are insects?

- How can they be beneficial to the world around us?

- What can we do to reduce their harmful effects?

What role do beetles play?

When creating PowerPoint or other types of slide presentations, be careful not to get carried away by inserting too many graphics.

The information should be presented as a bulleted list of facts, graphs, charts, and pictures or clip art to enhance the presentation of your answer to your question or solution to the problem. The slides are like the illustrations in a book. The illustrations enhance the story, but they don't tell the whole story. The slides should be visually appealing to your audience. The use of color, sound, and movement within the slides should be kept to a minimum, so that they don't distract from the information on the slides or from you as the presenter.

Recognizing and Avoiding Plagiarism

Plagiarism is a very serious form of cheating. It is the same as when you look at someone else's test paper and copy answers onto your paper. Plagiarism is when you use someone else's ideas as your own. These ideas could include written words, data, photographs, artwork, music, choreography for a dance, songs, videos, and movies. It also includes plans or architectural designs for a building, designs for a dress, shoes, and jewelry. The use of someone else's words in an oral presentation is also plagiarism if you do not quote the person or cite the person as a source of information.

Plagiarism is like cheating in an exam. You should not use someone else's answers, so why would you steal someone else's work?

Consequences of plagiarism

Teachers are usually pretty good at catching plagiarism. The most common method is simply to talk to other teachers and get ideas on where the work may have come from. There are other methods as well, including free software. Many schools have rules and punishments for students who cheat. The consequence of plagiarizing, even accidentally, can be failing an assignment, failing a class, being expelled from school, or losing your job. To avoid any question of plagiarism, it is best to take careful notes and always credit your sources. When in doubt as to whether or not you should credit a source, it is best to do so.

Accidental plagiarism

Plagiarism is not always something done on purpose. You can avoid the chance of plagiarizing by not paraphrasing when you are taking notes during the research process. Only write down facts. Then when you create your own paper or presentation, you will be using your own words. If you do use someone else's thoughts in writing, you must use quotation marks around those thoughts to show that they are not your own. It is important to copy quotations carefully and record the pages they come from when taking notes in order to credit, or cite, your source.

Fair use

Let's say that *Star Wars* is your favorite movie. You are not allowed to make a recording of *Star Wars* and sell it to a friend. You are also not allowed to take the script, shoot a new version of the movie, and try to release it as a new movie. However, if you are writing a research paper on science-fiction movies, you are allowed to quote small parts of the movie. If you are doing a presentation, you can show parts of the movie as part of your presentation. This is known as fair use. If you have questions about whether or not something is considered fair use, discuss it with your librarian or teacher.

The Internet and file sharing may be changing some of the rules of fair use. Before posting any comments, writing, or images on a website, it is important that you find out what the rules of the site are. With some websites putting your writing online may mean you give the site permission to use that writing in any way they want. Read all regulations and any sort of waivers carefully before posting your work online. When using something you have found online, it is always better to give too much credit rather than risk not giving enough.

Citations

Using a bibliography, footnotes (listed at the bottom of each page), and endnotes (listed at the end of a chapter, article, or book) are other ways to avoid plagiarism. The information you need in order to create a bibliography, footnote, or endnote is found on your source and fact note cards. It is important to make sure you list all the sources of your information. The note cards will be used to remind you which sources you have paraphrased and which you have quoted directly.

Note cards will also become the source of information for your bibliography. A bibliography, or list of works cited, is a list of sources used during research. Each type of source has its own way to be cited, but all entries contain basic information like the author, title, place of publication, publisher, and date of publication. Some sources, like encyclopedia and magazine articles and Web pages, need additional information for their bibliography entries. You need to enter any source used, whether written, oral, video, or audio, into your bibliography.

Examples of bibliographic entries

Book
Author last name, first name. Title of book. Place of publication: Publisher, copyright date.

Magazine/Newspaper
Author last name, first name. "Title of article." Title of magazine/newspaper. Date: Page number(s).

Encyclopedia
Article author last name, first name. "Title of article." Title of encyclopedia. Volume. Place of publication: Publisher, copyright date.

Website
Author last name, first name. "Title of the article." Title of the Web page. Copyright date or revision date. Publisher of Web page. Day month year you saw the site. Web address.

There are many different ways of creating bibliographies. Make sure to talk to your teacher about what method you should use.

Marking a citation in the text of a paragraph

Footnotes and endnotes must be listed numerically and consecutively in your essay. Footnote numbers must be superscripted (raised). In your text, add a superscripted number immediately after the quote or reference cited with no space. Here are some examples:

"There are some topics where you may already know many facts because of your previous experiences.[1] You may be only slightly familiar with some topics, and therefore only have a few facts about the topic. **You will first decide what you already know about your subject.**[2] These facts will go in the first column of the KWL chart. You will then need to determine what information you still need to find out. **These questions will go in the second column of the chart.**[3]**"**

Footnote entries at bottom of page

[From a book]
   [6] Sigmund Freud, Totem and Taboo (New York: Random House, 1918), 17.

[From an encyclopedia]
   [8] Lawrence A. Presley, "DNA Fingerprinting," World Book Encyclopedia, 2000 ed.

[From an article from a newspaper or magazine]
   [10] Michael Friscolanti, "Convicts 'Morally' Fit to Vote: Supreme Court Ruling," National Post [Toronto], 1 Nov. 2002: A4.

[From a Web page]
   [19] Canada, Indian and Northern Affairs, "Aboriginal Peoples Survey: From APS I to APS II." Facts from Stats, Corporate Information Management Directorate, Issue No. 15, Mar. 2000, Dec. 15, 2004 <http://www.inac.gc.ca/nr/nwltr/sts/2000-03_e.html>.

A Rough Draft

Before writing a rough draft of your presentation, you will compare your note cards to your graphic organizer or outline in order to finalize your graphic organizer or outline. You may decide that you will need to add or discard topics or subtopics based on the information you have gathered during your research. After you have created your final graphic organizer or outline and determined that you have enough relevant information to answer your question or solve your problem, it is time to begin writing a rough draft of your presentation. A rough draft is the first time you try to put all of your information down. It is for your use only. However, you should keep a copy of it to refer to later.

Writing a rough draft can be frustrating, but it is necessary to create a good presentation or report.

Editing

Once you have completed your rough draft, you will need to edit it. You begin this process by reading your draft, looking to make sure that what you have written relates back to the original research question or problem and follows your graphic organizer or outline. You will make corrections where you find errors or the need for additional information. You should not be concerned about correct spellings and punctuation at this time. Make sure to keep your note cards, because you may need to refer to them as you make changes.

Now it is time for you to share your draft with a classmate, parent, tutor, or teacher. The classmate will read your draft presentation, looking to make sure the introduction clearly states the question or problem to be solved, that there are enough supporting details, and that the conclusion clearly states the answer to the question or solution to the problem. Your classmate will note corrections or additions he or she thinks you will want to make. If you have been working on a paper for a long time, you may find it difficult to take suggestions from others. However, it is important to try to keep an open mind. A fresh set of eyes can help you see errors and think of new ideas.

After you have considered the corrections suggested by your classmate, you will want to correct any misspelled words and check for correct punctuation. It is helpful to have someone like a parent review your draft to check for problems as well. If you have been working on a paper for a long time, it can be hard to see errors.

Multiple drafts

In school, teachers often give assignments including the specific number of drafts you need to write. Other times it's up to you. There is no perfect number of drafts. In general, you should make sure you have left enough time to have three or four drafts. As you gain more experience in research and writing, you will find how many drafts work best for you. The number may change depending on the type of assignment you are doing.

Summary

Every day you receive information. Before you can prepare a research project, you have to learn how to organize the information you have found. You will also have to decide the best way to present your information.

Graphic organizers and outlines

Graphic organizers are especially helpful for students who are visual learners. KWL charts can help you combine what you already know on the topic with the new information you learn during the research process. Other graphic organizers, like concept webs, graphic outlines, and problem-solving organizers, can help organize your facts so that you can create a logical presentation. Concept webs are groups of bubbles. These bubbles are arranged so that similar information is grouped together, but there is no order to them.

Graphic outlines also group similar information together but are structured so that the facts are in a logical order, making it easy to write paragraphs or essays. Graphic outlines use a numbering system that arranges your facts in a logical order. Problem-solving organizers, like concept webs, help you arrange your facts in bubbles, but the bubbles follow an order like the graphic outline.

Critical-thinking skills and problem solving

Some of your research questions or problems will require you to use critical-thinking and problem-solving skills. When you use critical-thinking skills, you are using your facts to draw conclusions and make inferences. Critical thinkers look at information with clarity, accuracy, and common sense and make assumptions based on the information. Once your assumptions have been made, you will be able to answer your research question and be able to communicate it to your audience. You will use critical-thinking and problem-solving skills on a daily basis in your lifetime.

Oral presentations

Some presentations may be given orally. These presentations might be a speech or a debate. In order to give a successful oral presentation, you should first prepare it as a written report or essay. Oral presentations may include any of the small-group formats to be used as visual support for the facts in your presentation or as handouts. Oral presentations may also be computer generated using a software program.

You use critical-thinking skills in many everyday situations, even in a grocery store.

Plagiarism

Plagiarism is a serious offense. When you plagiarize you present someone else's words or thoughts as your own. Plagiarism is a form of cheating, even if it is done accidentally. You are allowed to copy small portions of an author's text or use an artist's image, song, or video as part of your paper or oral presentation. This is called fair use. If you are unsure of what is allowed and not allowed, you should ask your librarian or teacher.

When you first start preparing a report or presentation, all the information can seem overwhelming. Knowing some techniques for organizing and using information can help make the process smoother.

Glossary

Arabic number   most common symbol used to represent a number. Examples of Arabic numbers are 1, 10, 100.

biased   prejudiced, or with an inclination toward a particular point of view

bibliography   list citing each source used in researching a topic

cite   give credit to a work or author

concept web   diagram that shows the relationship among ideas. Concept webs are also sometimes called graphic organizers.

critical thinking   process of locating, evaluating, analyzing, and using information gathered from more than one source in order to solve a problem

data   collection of information

database   searchable collection of information that is stored electronically

endnote   note placed with others in a list at the end of a report that gives the source of a quote or paraphrase of information used in writing the report

fishbone map   diagram that shows details of a main idea

flip book   small book consisting of a series of sheets of paper folded to create pages of different widths or lengths

flowchart   diagram that shows step-by-step progression using connecting lines

footnote   note placed at the bottom of the page of a report that gives the source of a quote or paraphrase of information found on that page

graph   visual comparison of similar information about two or more objects

graphic   presented visually

graphic organizer   diagram that shows the relationships among ideas

graphic outline   method of organizing information using a combination of numbers and letters to indicate the main topics, as well as the subtopics under each main point

imprint page   page found in the front of a book that lists publishing information

KWL chart   table that helps to show what a person **K**nows about a topic, what the person **W**ants to know about the topic, and what the person **L**earns about the topic

oral   spoken

paraphrase   restatement of a fact found in a resource that is put into one's own words

plagiarism   claiming of someone else's words or thoughts as your own

problem solving   ability to define a problem, identify and prioritize possible solutions and their consequences, and then select a solution to solve a problem

problem-solving model   diagram that states a problem, identifies and prioritizes possible solutions and their consequences, and then shows the solution to the problem

Roman numeral   method used in ancient Rome to represent numbers by using letters of the alphabet. For example, I is the symbol for 1, X is the symbol for 10, and C is the symbol for 100.

rough draft   first attempt at writing a paper, usually improved upon and discarded

statistics   collection of information or data

summary   shortened version of information

topic sentence   sentence that states the main point of a paragraph

Venn diagram   graphic organizer that uses circles or squares that cross each other to show the areas that two or more things have in common, and the areas where they are different

visual organizer   diagram that uses geometric shapes like circles, rectangles, or squares. These shapes, with information in them, are connected by lines that group like, or similar, information together.

Find Out More

Books

Career Skills Library: Research and Information Management.
New York: Ferguson, 2004.

Chin, Beverly. *How to Write a Great Research Paper.* San
Francisco: Jossey Bass, 2004.

Gaines, Ann Graham. *Don't Steal Copyrighted Stuff.* Berkeley
Heights, NJ: Enslow, 2008.

Websites

www.lib.colostate.edu/teen_research/
This site from the Colorado State University provides tips for
students doing research.

www.liunet.edu/cwis/cwp/library/workshop/citmla.htm
MLA Citation Style: *MLA Handbook for Writers of Research
Papers*, 6th edition. Long Island University.

www.graphic.org
This site gives several examples of graphic organizers and
discusses how they are useful.

Further Research

Fair use and file sharing

Review the information on fair use and file sharing on page 37. Find examples of websites that take contributions or photos from readers. Can you find any information explaining who owns the rights to the information posted online?

Venn diagrams

Review the section on Venn diagrams on page 8. Who was John Venn, and why did he invent this diagram? What is the largest Venn diagram you can find an example of?

Debates

Review the section on debates on page 32. What are some famous debates in history? How have debates influenced political contests? What are some of the rules used in debates?

Garbage and recycling

Review pages 24–27. What is your town's recycling program? Is it effective? Where does the trash that you throw away end up?

Index